Popcorn

LEVEL 4

/or/oi/

DECODABLES BY jump!

Teaching Tips

Blue Level 4

This book focuses on the phonemes **/or/oi/**.

Before Reading

- Discuss the title. Ask readers what they think the book will be about. Have them briefly explain why.
- Ask readers to sort the words on page 3. Read the sounds and words together.

Read the Book

- Encourage readers to break down unfamiliar words into units of sound. Then, ask them to string the sounds together to create the words.
- Urge readers to point out when the focused phonics phonemes appear in the text.

After Reading

- Encourage children to reread the book independently or with a friend.
- Ask readers to name other words with /or/ or /oi/ phonemes. On a separate sheet of paper, have them write the words out.

5357 Penn Avenue South
Minneapolis, MN 55419
www.jumplibrary.com

Decodables by Jump! are published by Jump! Library.

Library of Congress Cataloging-in-Publication Data is available at www.loc.gov or upon request from the publisher.

ISBN: 979-8-88996-831-3 (hardcover)
ISBN: 979-8-88996-832-0 (paperback)
ISBN: 979-8-88996-833-7 (ebook)

Photo Credits

Images are courtesy of Shutterstock.com. With thanks to Getty Images, Thinkstock Photo and iStockphoto. Cover – SizeSquares. 4–5 – Anatoliy Karlyuk, ViDI Studio. 6–7 – New Africa, Suteren. 8–9 – Faisal JTM, Krakenimages.com. 10–11 – Melica, Valdis Muiznieks. 12–13 – Mandy Creighton, Mauricio Graiki. 14–15 – Monkey Business Images, Nerza. 16 – Shutterstock.

Can you sort all the words on this page into two groups?

Coil

Pork

Words with

or

Horn

Join

Foil

North

Words with

oi

Soil

Cork

You can pop corn with a pot and some oil.

Get a pot. It will need to be big so that the corn can puff up.

Get some oil. Tip a little bit of oil in the big pot.

Have Mom or Dad help you get the pot on the stove.

Oil can get hot. Do not let the oil spit out at you.

Get some corn. Do not boil the corn. Get it in the hot oil.

Get a lid on the pot. The corn will pop a lot.

Pop pop pop. The corn will jump in the pot.

If you do not have a lid, you will have to sort out a mess.

Quick, there is too much! Tell Mom or Dad to get it off the stove.

Get some popcorn with your hand or a fork.

Sit with Mom and Dad and eat up all the popcorn.

Sound out each word. Does it have an /or/ or /oi/ sound?

sports

toilet

stork

coin